Welcome Back to Musi

Let's review our notes and bow hold.

Be sure to follow your teacher's directions.

Open String Review

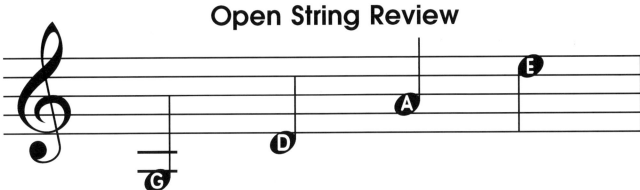

The Bow Hold

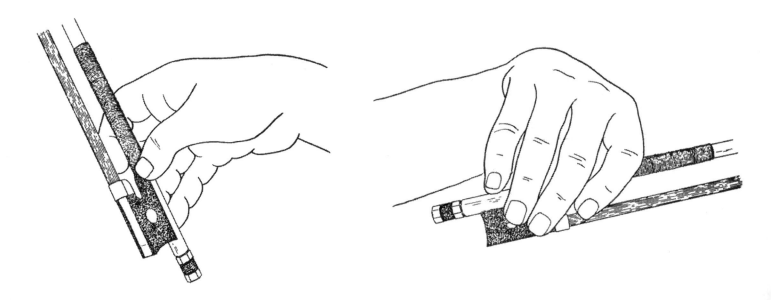

Note Review

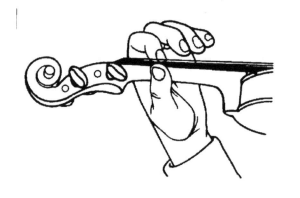

First finger on "D"

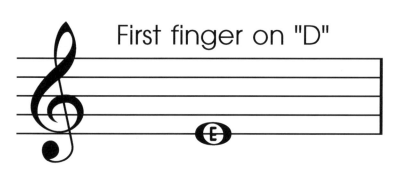

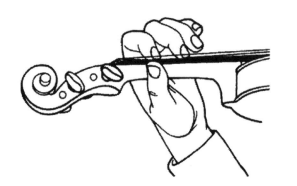

First & second fingers on "D"

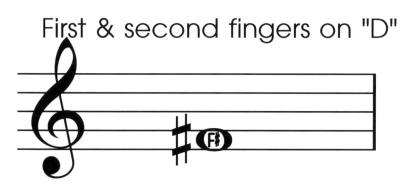

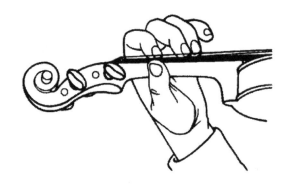

First, second & third fingers on "D"

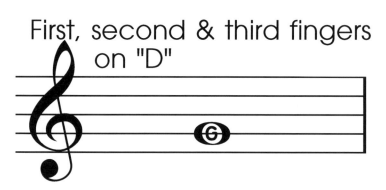

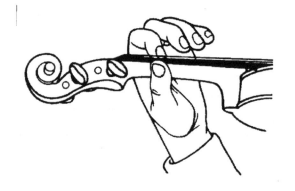

First finger on "A"

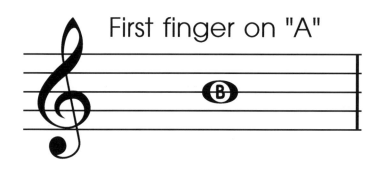

Au Claire de la Lune

Hot Cross Buns

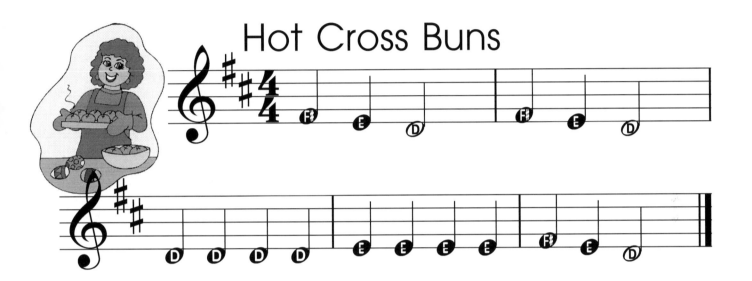

Good King Wenceslas

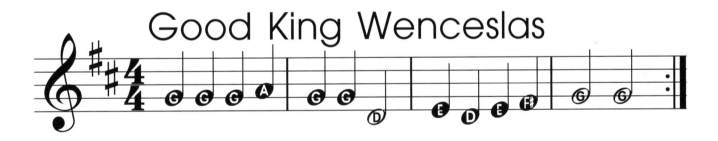

Mary Had a Little Lamb

4

Lightly Row

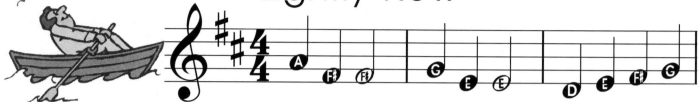

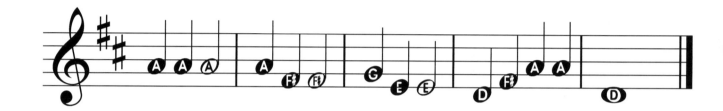

Aura Lee

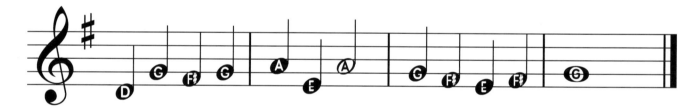

Go Tell Aunt Rhody

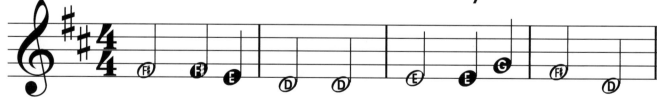

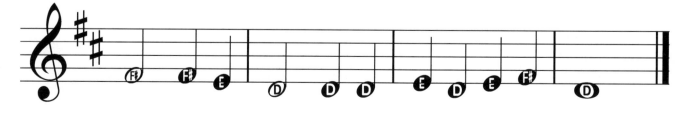

Frog Song

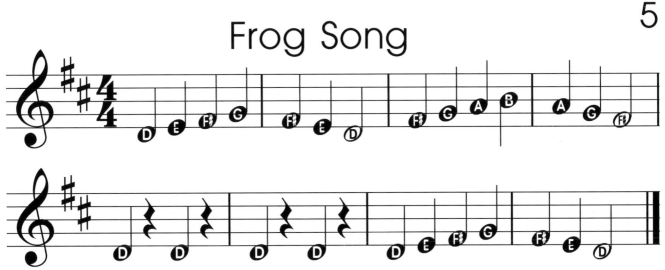

Camptown Races

London Bridge

Dreydl, Dreydl

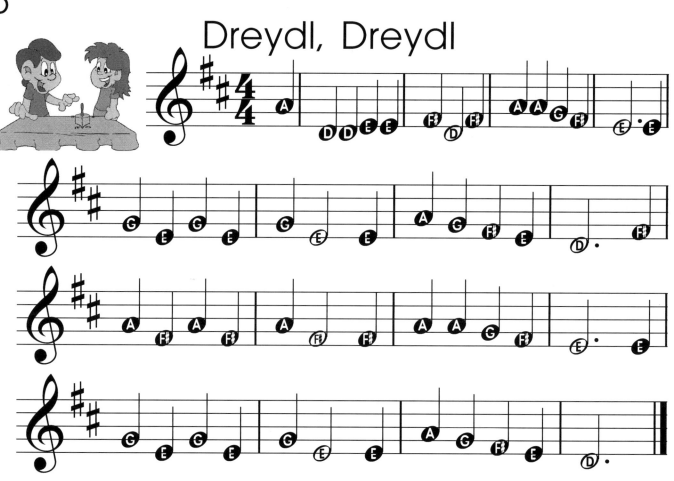

Twinkle, Twinkle, Little Star

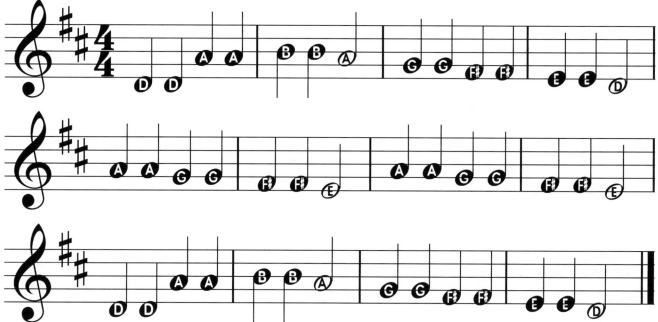

Jolly Old St. Nicholas

The Bridge at Avignon

Pop Goes the Weasel

Jingle Bells

Are You Sleeping?

Musette

10

Lo Yisa Goy

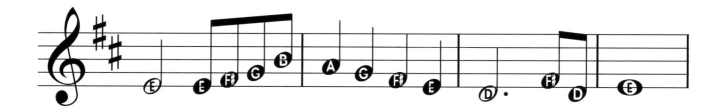

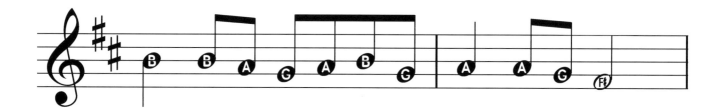

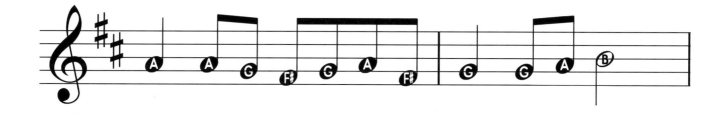

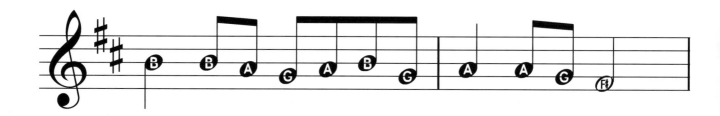

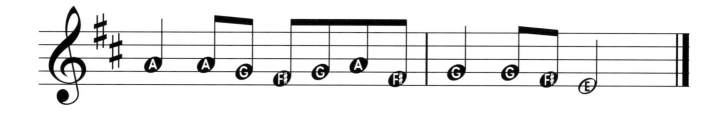

Baa Baa Black Sheep

Symphony No.1 by Brahms

This Little Light of Mine

Up on the House Top

This Old Man

Old MacDonald

14 Spring Theme from the Four Seasons

Rock-a-my-Soul

Largo from New World Symphony

16

Kum Ba Yah

Ode to Joy

Oh, Susana

Shepherd's Hey

18

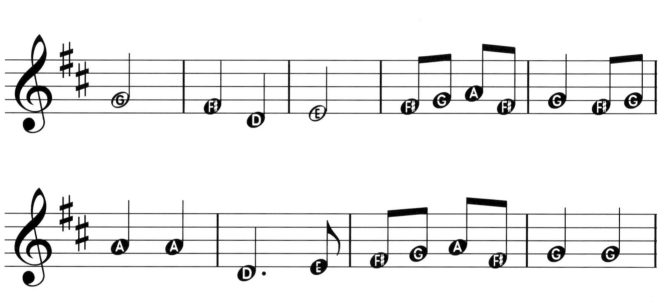

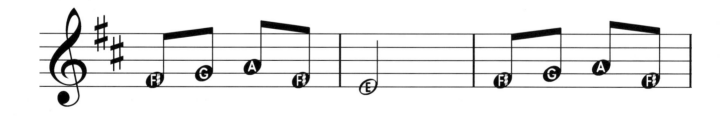

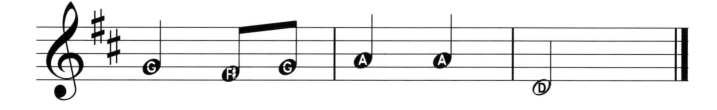

More Note Review and Exercises

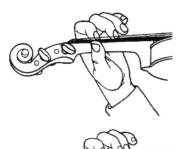

C SHARP

Two fingers on "A"

HIGH D

Three fingers on "A"

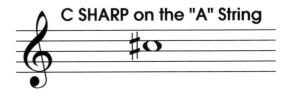

C SHARP on the "A" String

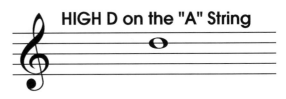

HIGH D on the "A" String

The D Major Scale

Catch Those Notes!

20

Slippery Stuff

Rootin' Tootin'

Marchin' Along

Jazzy Wazzy

22

OPEN "E" STRING

1.

2.

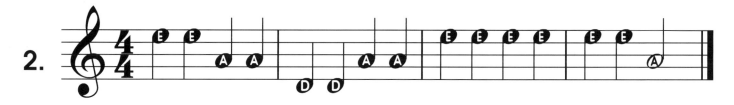

"F" SHARP

First finger on E string

3.

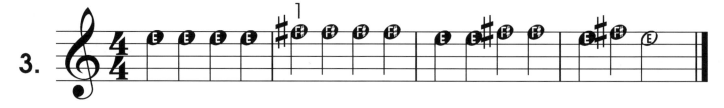

4.

5.

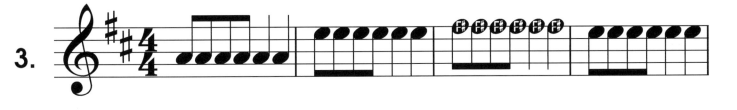

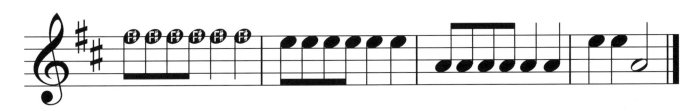

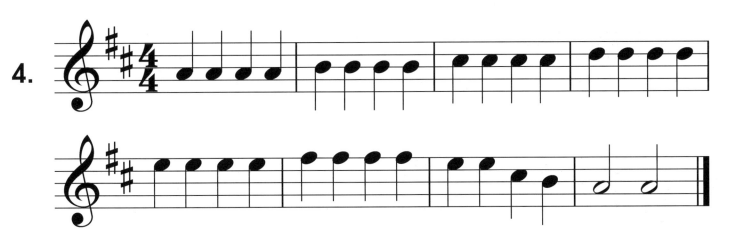

24

"G SHARP"

NEW!

NEW NOTE

Second finger on E string

1.

2.

3.

4.

5.

1.

2.

3.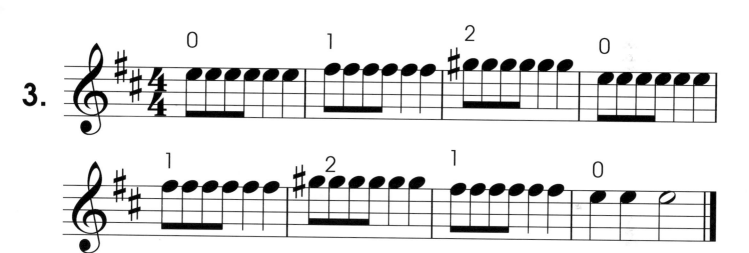

Three sharps in the key
signature includes G sharp.

Mary Had A Little Lamb

1.

2.

3.
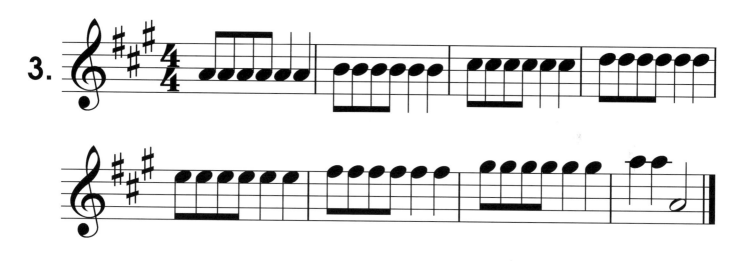

4.

HIGH "B"

NEW NOTE

Fourth finger on E string

1.

2.

3.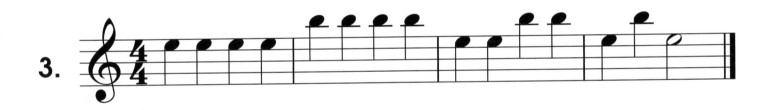

4.

5.

Songs in the Key of "E"

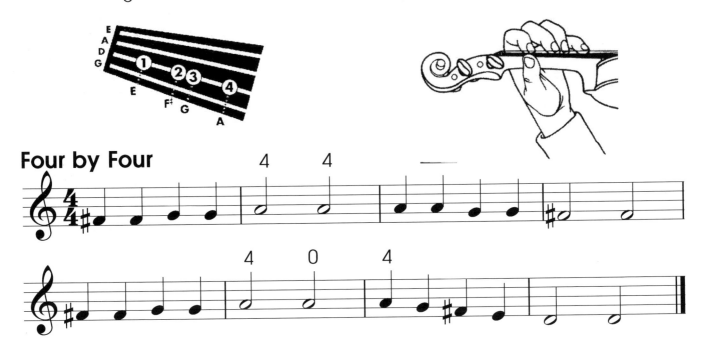

Your 4th finger is often used to match the pitch of the next highest open string, creating a smoother tone and fewer changes between strings for bowing.

Four by Four

4th Finger Marathon

This Old Man

OPEN "G" STRING

NEW NOTE

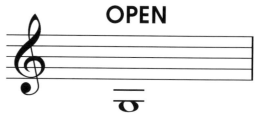

OPEN

1.

2.

"Low A" on G string

NEW NOTE

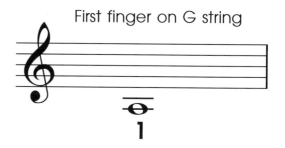

First finger on G string

1

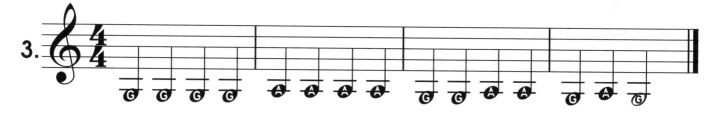

3.   G G G G   A A A A   G G A A   G A G

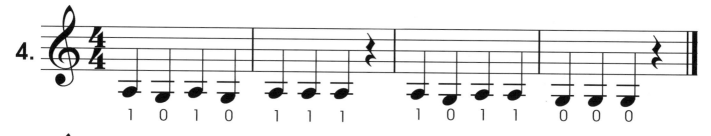

4.   1 0 1 0   1 1 1   1 0 1 1   0 0 0

5.

"LOW B" on G string

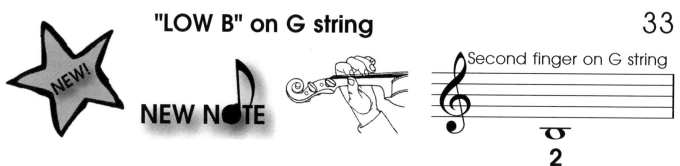

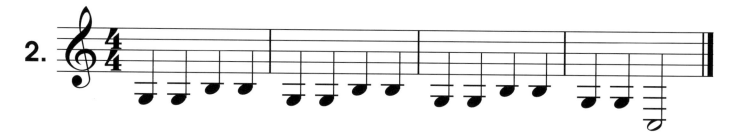

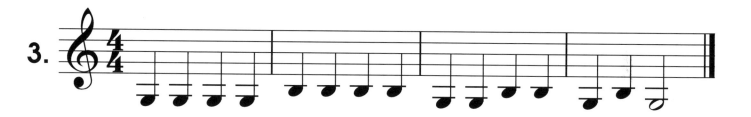

34

1.

2.

3.

Mary Had A Little Lamb

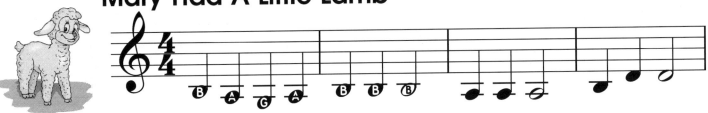

"C" on the "G" string

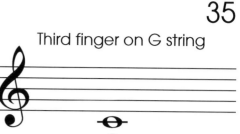

Third finger on G string

NEW!

NEW NOTE

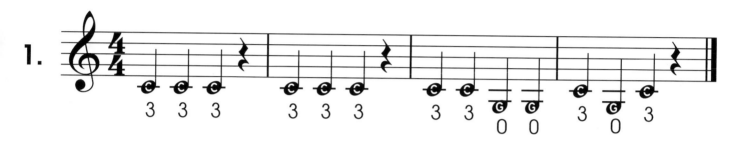

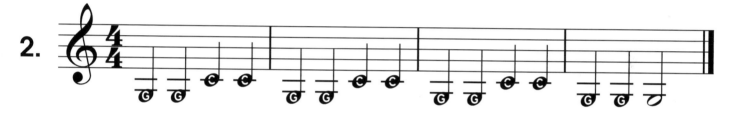

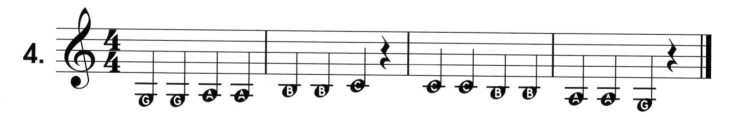

36

"D" on the "G" string

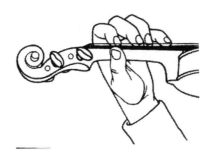

Fourth finger on G string

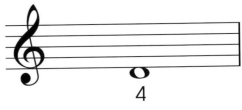

Fingers on the "G" String

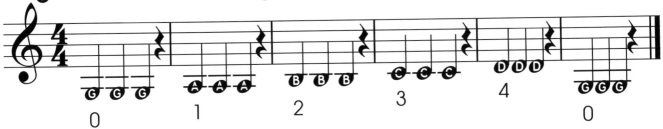

Scotland's Burning

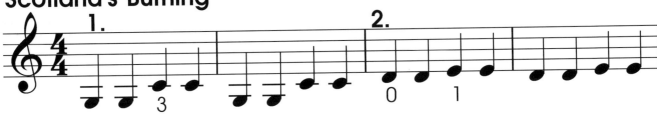

G Major Scale

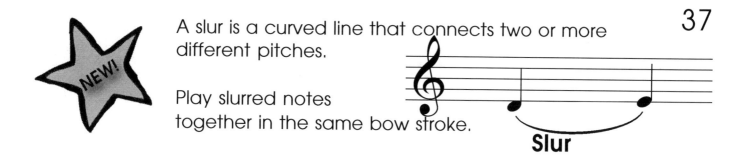

A slur is a curved line that connects two or more different pitches.

Play slurred notes together in the same bow stroke.

Slur

Slurring Along

Russian Folk Song

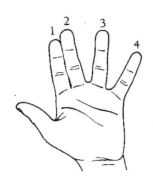

Low 2nd Finger

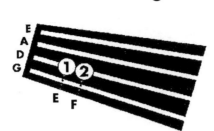

"F" Natural
Low second finger on "D" string

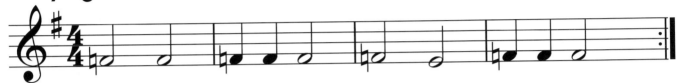

L2

Playing "F" Natural

Hot Cross Buns

4 3 L2

The Snake Charmer

L2

4

4

4

Low 2nd Finger

Low second finger on "A" string

Playing "C" Natural

Hot Cross Buns

The Snake Charmer

40

Half Step Song on "D"

Half Step Song on "A"

C Major Scale

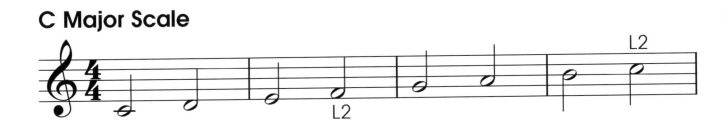

Sakura

42

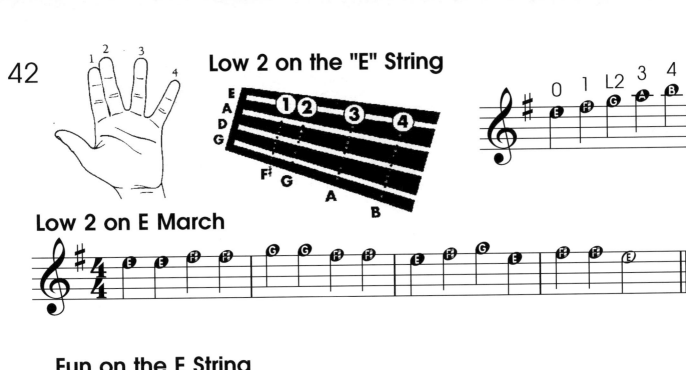

Low 2 on the "E" String

Low 2 on E March

Fun on the E String

G Major Scale

Finale from the "New World Symphony"

Simple Gifts

Rhythm Fun

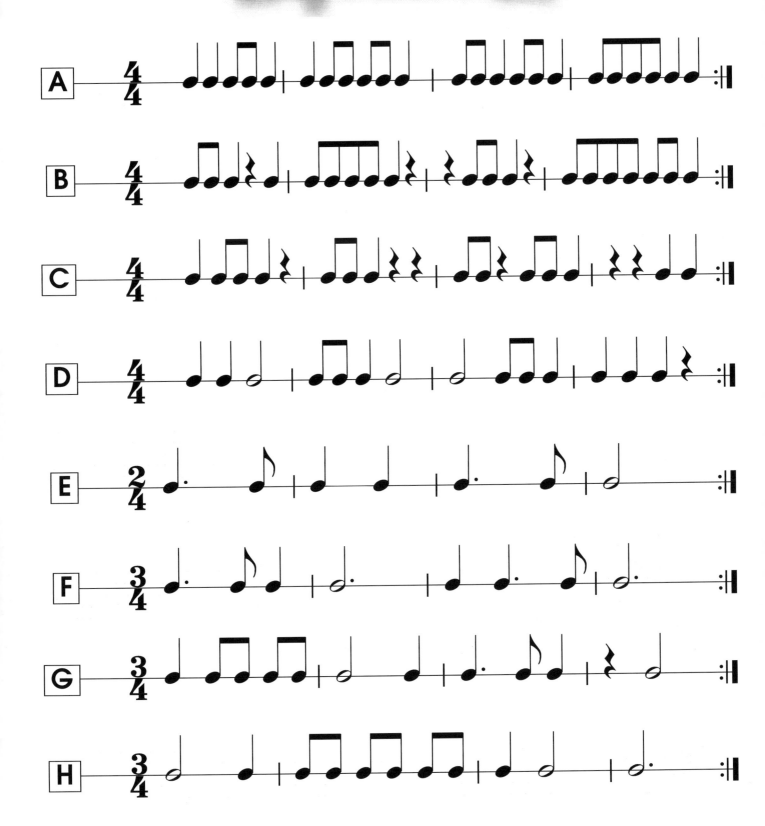

Fun Work

Write in the letters to these notes.

Notes on the D string only.

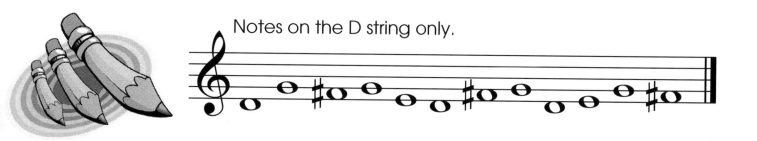

Notes on the A string only.

Notes on the E string only.

Notes on the G string only.

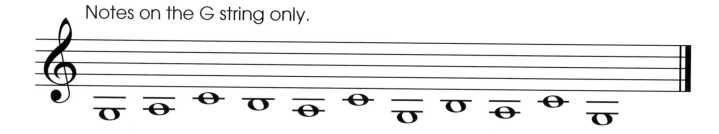

Notes on any of the four strings.

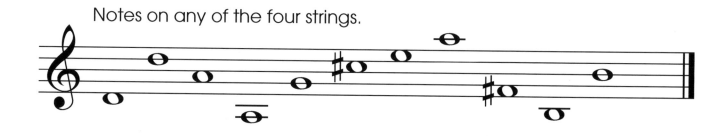

Made in the USA
Middletown, DE
12 December 2016